COMPANION TO

SAINT PAUL

by
J.B. Midgley

*All booklets are published thanks to the
generous support of the members of the
Catholic Truth Society*

CATHOLIC TRUTH SOCIETY
PUBLISHERS TO THE HOLY SEE

CONTENTS

INTRODUCTION

The Report 'Evangelisation in England and Wales' commissioned by the Bishops' Conference in 2002, responds to Pope John Paul II's statement that the dawn of a millennium is an appropriate time to proclaim the Gospel with renewed confidence. It reminds Christians that their Baptism calls them to continue the mission which Christ gave to the Apostles to make disciples of all nations in the name of the Holy Trinity. The authors recommend that a refreshed evangelism might begin with a personal affirmation of faith nurtured by continued religious education, prayer, and scripture-study groups in the parish community.

Saint Paul, the shining model of evangelism who "opened the door of faith to the pagans", helps successive generations show themselves to be "the friends of the Lord by making known the glorious splendours of His reign", especially by the example of lives conducted in the spirit of faith. The same Jesus who met him on the road to Damascus, visits them in their hearts, inspires them with the power of the Holy Spirit, and promises that He will never leave them.

Paul is the fearless witness who longs for all peoples to find faith in Christ who rebuilt the Temple of His Body after it had been torn down by death. The ruthless persecutor has become the ardent persuader who takes the Good News to the corners of the earth as a minister of his Lord's grace. He is a monumental figure in the history of Christianity, the development of the universal Church, and in the religious education of successive generations. The 'Acts of the Apostles' and Paul's Letters, especially when read in their entirety, reveal a powerful advocate who is eager to help disciples as they follow the path he traces for them, and it is hoped these pages offer a helpful accompaniment (cf. *Ac* 14:18; *Ps* 144).

J.B. Midgley,
Downham Market,
Solemnity of Saints Peter and Paul, June 29th 2003.

LEGACY OF SAINT PAUL

Our Lord said that "salvation comes from the Jews" and it was among the people of Israel that He entered humanity, called His Apostles and chose Paul, "the Hebrew of the Hebrews", to ensure that a new spiritual Israel would embrace not only Jews but the whole human race. The Law of Moses was a written law which emphasised attention to the details of ritual and prescriptions, but God writes a New Law in the hearts of all His people whom he has gathered to Himself in Christ. They are empowered by the Holy Spirit and given the grace which sanctifies their souls through faith and charity.

Paul's enduring message is about the freedom which Christ brings to God's people in whom He lives, and which He has achieved by His sacrifice on the Cross with the Holy Spirit and in charity. It is a freedom so unrestrained that the opportunities to serve Him are limitless. The abuse of free-will to make the better choice which prompted the initial disobedience in Eden brought sin and death into the world, with an unease which no pursuit of self-satisfaction can assuage. Christ's moral law gives a joyous freedom and peace because its observance in love and with the Holy Spirit rids us of evil, the pangs of conscience and, ultimately, of the Law itself because precepts are obeyed through love, not fear. "If you keep my commandments", Our Lord says, "you will remain in my love... so that my own joy may be in you and your joy be complete." (*Jn* 15:9-11). Paul tells the Philippians that now everyone is to be happy in the Lord. "There is no need to wrorry, but if there is anything you need, pray for it with thanksgiving, and that peace of God which is so much greater than we can understand, will guard your hearts and your thoughts." It is true that, of themselves, the deeds by which we are judged are incapable of saving us, but there is no need to fear because Christ crucified has made them meritorious by the living faith He brings from the Father, and by uniting us all in Him. The Law is now completed by love and we are saved by the faith which is expressed in the works of love.

Paul teaches that the Body of Christ is present both in the Church and in the Eucharist. Christians constitute this one Body, united as members with their Head. The One Bread of the Eucharist is a participation in His Body and reinforces union with Him. He sees this sharing of life with the Lord and other believers as physical rather than metaphoric. Christ and His Bride, the Church, are the fullness of one person in a unity of such close reality that it can be called His Body, and He is the head from whom the members are nourished. We find salvation when we use our lips to say that Jesus is Lord, and our hearts to believe that God has raised Him from the dead. We have received the Spirit of adoption so that, as His children, we are able to call God Abba, Father and, as His heirs, we share Christ's inheritance, participating in His sufferings and His glory. (cf. *1 Co* 10:16ff; *Rm* 8:14-17, 10:8-10, 12:5; *Eph*; *Col*).

Those who doubt their personal qualifications to carry the Gospel, may be comforted that, at first glance, Paul seems an unlikely addition to the ranks of the Apostles. This Pharisee, who was a legal adviser to the hostile Sanhedrin, a cruelly efficient persecutor of Christ's followers, and a citizen of an occupying foreign power could be opinionated, short-tempered, censorious, and disruptive, but he became consumed with love for Christ and his Church whose members he referred to tenderly as his "little children". Though he trembled at the thought of speaking in public, he did so with a certainty that the Lord would make good his deficiencies. He showed heroic courage in the face of danger and welcomed the severity of sufferings which united him with those of Christ whom he followed to the death, rejoicing in His Resurrection. Today we pray to the Lord: "Direct each thought, each effort of our life, so that the limits of our faults and weaknesses may not obscure the vision of your glory or keep us from the peace you have promised."

DEVOTION TO SAINT PAUL

The Universal Church honours Saints Peter and Paul with a Vigil on June 28th and a Solemnity on the 29th when Catholics are expected to attend the celebration of Mass. The shared Feast is an indication of opinion in the early Church that they were martyred about the same time, even the same day. When Rome was devastated by fire in AD 64, the emperor Nero blamed the Christians who by this time had become a group distinguishable from the synagogue. According to the Roman historian Tacitus ('Annals' 15), Nero ordered the conflagration himself, but Peter and Paul were among the victims of the subsequent persecution. The first pope to adopt the Apostle's name was St Paul I (757-767) who is remembered for safeguarding the position of the Papal States which his predecessor, Pope Stephen II, had received from Pepin, King of the Franks. He resisted the iconoclasm of the emperor Constantine V and restored the churches in Rome to which he translated the relics of many saints from the catacombs.

Before the re-ordering of the Roman Calendar in 1969, Saint Paul had a personal commemoration on June 30th but this has been incorporated in the remembrance of his conversion on January 25th, which appropriately concludes the Church's annual Octave of Prayer for

Christian Unity. He is the Patron Saint of Greece, Malta, and the city of London. In England forty-three churches were dedicated to him and, with Saint Peter, another two hundred and eighty three, but perhaps it is his cathedral in London which best exemplifies the great Apostle's enduring influence. In AD 604, only eight years after Saint Augustine brought Christianity to England, King Ethelbert built a church dedicated to Saint Paul in London. This became the seat of the first bishop of the East Saxons, the Roman abbot Saint Mellitus whom Pope St Gregory had sent with Augustine and who now lies buried with him in the Cathedral Church of Saints Peter and Paul in Canterbury, England's ecclesiastical capital. When the church was destroyed by fire, it was rebuilt by Saint Erkenwald, bishop from 675 to 685, but this was demolished by the Vikings on one of their regular invasions. After its successor was again overtaken by fire in 1087, a new Norman building, "Old Saint Paul's", was completed in 1240. The addition of a Gothic choir in 1313 made it the third longest church in Europe and the one with the tallest spire. It survived being struck by lightning, and the vandalism which occurred during the Tudor period of reformation, to became a centre of trade where merchants sold their wares in the nave.

During the Civil War, the Cathedral was commandeered by Parliamentary troops for use as a cavalry barracks, but fortunes revived with the

Restoration of the Monarchy in 1660 when Charles II instructed Christopher Wren to undertake major refurbishment. The architect had hardly begun when the Great Fire of London in 1666 reduced Old Saint Paul's to ashes and rubble. With the authority of a Royal Warrant, Wren commenced building a new Saint Paul's in 1675. When he was salvaging stones from the old for the centre of the new, he noticed that one of them bore the Latin "Resurgam", "I shall rise again", and he had the word inscribed on the base of the south door beneath a carved phoenix, a happy reminder of the Apostle's confidence in Christ's Resurrection. Saint Paul's was completed in 1708, the building having taken only thirty-three years which means that, alone among English cathedrals, it is the result of one man's vision.

From the Liturgy

"God our Father, you taught the Gospel to all the world through the preaching of Paul your Apostle. May we who celebrate his conversion to the faith follow him in bearing witness to your truth, and experience the power of his intercession." (Opening Prayer, January 25th, and Collect, June 30th, adapted.)

Disciples throughout time can hear Jesus' words to Paul on the Damascus road as addressed to themselves. "I have appeared to you to appoint you as my servant; you are to tell the others what you have seen of me today and what I will show you in the future. I will save you from the people of Israel and from the Gentiles to whom I will send you. You are to open their eyes and turn them from the darkness to the light, and from the power of Satan to God, so that through their faith in me they will have their sins forgiven and receive their place among God's chosen people" (*Ac* 26:16-18).

"Everywhere he was beaten, insulted and reviled. He treated it all as if it were a triumphal procession, setting up trophies of victory everywhere on earth, giving thanks to God saying, 'Thanks be to God who in Christ always leads to triumph' ...He was rich with the love of Christ which was the greatest of all things to him. While he had this he reckoned himself the most blessed of men... To find this love was joy; this to him was life; it was the whole world,... the kingdom,... the promise... Death and a thousand torments he thought of as child's play, provided only he could endure something for Christ's sake." (Second Homily on St Paul, St John Chrysostom, Office of Readings, January 25th.)

"Out of His infinite glory, may He give you the power through His spirit for your hidden self to grow strong, so that Christ may live in your hearts through faith, and then planted in love and built on love, you will with all the saints have strength to grasp the breadth and the length, the height and the depth until, knowing the love of Christ which is beyond all knowledge, you are filled with the utter fullness of God. Glory be to Him whose power working in us, can do infinitely more than we can ask or imagine; glory be to Him from generation to generation in the Church and in Christ Jesus for ever and ever. Amen." (Saint Paul's own prayer, *Ep* 3:14-20.)

> "From heaven's height Christ spoke to call
> The Gentiles' great Apostle Paul
> Whose doctrine like the thunder sounds
> To the wide world's remotest bounds;
>
> The Word's great seed abroad he flings;
> Straightway a mighty harvest springs,
> And fruits of holy deeds supply
> God's everlasting granary.
>
> The lamp his burning faith displays
> Has filled the world with glorious rays;
> The realm of darkness is o'erthrown,
> That Christ may reign and reign alone."
> (*'Paule doctor egregie'*, St Peter Damian, 1007-72.)

In the apocryphal 'Acts of Paul and Thecla', the second century Roman writer Onesiphoros describes Paul as "rather short, balding, bow-legged, with joined eyebrows and a hooked nose," a candid portraiture softened by the detail that he was "strongly built, graceful and, at times, looked like an angel." It seems he suffered from a physical disorder, a "thorn in the flesh" which the Fathers of the Church suspect may have been a type of epilepsy. Whatever its nature, his achievements are extraordinary in the light of a condition he found distressing. (cf. *2 Co* 12:7). The single-mindedness which he brought to the persecution of Christians before his conversion, was afterwards seen in his love of Jesus Christ and in the total and selfless commitment with which he preached His Gospel. He never married, but celibacy did not preclude the warm personal relationships which are evident in his letters. In the first Letter to the Thessalonians, for example, he thanks God for the progress which his converts, his "pride and joy", are making in the Christian way of life, and praises them for the fine example they are giving to others. He has known them for only a few months but cannot wait to see them again and is overjoyed that they show the same eagerness to welcome him.

Saint Paul in Art

Paul's adventurous life of evangelisation which St Luke has described in the 'Acts of the Apostles', inspired artists to picture him holding a sword and a book, as in 'St Paul, the Holy Family and St George' by Giovanni Bellini (1430-1516) in the Venice Academy, and in the anonymous sculpture in the Toulouse Museum of Fine Arts. Frescoes in the Roman Catacombs reflect

Onesiphoros' description as does the icon by Andrei
Rublev (1407). In Michelangelo's Vatican fresco 'The
Conversion of Saul', Paul lies on the ground, thrown from
his horse, in a mediaeval symbol of fallen pride, as Christ
appears in the heavens escorted by three angels against a
background of mountains which enfolds a vision of the
new Jerusalem. A beam of light which follows the
contours of the figures is shaped like a bishop's crozier
evocative of Paul's destiny to be a shepherd of God's
people. A lightning flash of grace bathes his head as he
awakens to a new and inspired consciousness.

THE LIFE OF SAINT PAUL

Early Years

Tarsus, the capital of Cilicia on the Mediterranean coast of present-day Turkey then called Asia Minor, was classified as Roman for services to the empire's cause and enjoyed such cultural and commercial advantages that its citizens proudly stamped the descriptions "First, fairest and best", and "No mean city" on their coinage. Its language was Greek and, like many Graeco-Roman economic centres, it was home to one of the Jewish colonies which settled after the Israelite dispersion, the 'Diaspora' which had started with the Babylonian exile around BC 730. The future Apostle was born to the Pharisaic family of a successful tent and cloak manufacturer in this community about the same time as his future Lord. He was called Saul after the greatest man of his tribe of Benjamin, and later Paul by virtue of his inherited Roman citizenship. In addition to Greek which was spoken in the synagogues around the Mediterranean, he would learn the orthodox Jew's Aramaic, and would become fluent in Hebrew. Though he was raised according to strict Jewish tradition, his writings show that he was not unaffected by the Hellenised atmosphere of an affluent, pagan city with its military base, markets, theatres, temples and sports arenas.

Saul was highly intelligent, well-educated in Greek philosophy as well as the Jewish Scriptures, and his father arranged for him to stay with relatives in Jerusalem to graduate as a Master of the Law at the prestigious School of Hittel. This was an institution, founded by a leading rabbi during the reign of Herod the Great, where he was fortunate to have an eminent rabbi and Pharisee called Gamaliel as his tutor. As a Pharisee himself, Saul was zealous for the integrity of doctrine, tradition and the rigorous observance of the Mosaic Law, and became expert in the Jewish lore enshrined in the Talmud, and in the methods of exposition and debate which one day he would use to such effect in presenting the Gospel message. (cf. *Ac* 13:9; *Ph* 3:5.)

Saul's letters suggest that he returned to Tarsus to continue his legal studies and follow the directions of Gamaliel some time before John the Baptist began his mission to preach a baptism of penance for the forgiveness of sins. His would have been eager to teach in the school attached to his synagogue and, as a legal expert, was probably consulted by the Tarsus Sanhedrin of which, as yet, he was too young to be a member. His father trained him in the skills of his trade, using the Cilician fabric to manufacture tents and cloaks, so that he could conform to the Talmud's recommendation that "he who has a trade is like a vineyard that is fenced." He was able to earn his living in this way even on his missionary journeys and so illustrated the dignity of labour in an age when it was thought suitable only for slaves. (cf. *1 Co* 9:12.)

The Death of Stephen

While Saul remained in Tarsus, momentous events were happening in Palestine. The long-expected Messiah had come as promised, preached for three years and was then rejected, especially by the religious leaders of the Jews. Jesus' followers who had been devastated by his death were wonderfully strengthened by His Resurrection and by the coming of the Holy Spirit at Pentecost with His gifts. The Apostles were convinced that Israel had made a tragic mistake and were determined to bring the people back to their Lord and Saviour, but the religious professionals were not inclined to accept the advice of a motley crew of Galileans whose teaching was beginning to have a disruptive influence. In fact, the number of converts had grown so quickly that the Apostles appointed seven deacons to take charge of the distribution of alms, especially to widows, to preach, and to assist with general administration. One of them was Stephen, an eloquent young man who was learned in the Scriptures and Jewish history. When he was arrested on a trumped-up charge of blasphemy, he mounted a forceful defence of Christ's teaching, and pointed out that God is not dependent on the Temple which, like the Law of Moses, was a temporary institution awaiting the transformation brought by the Messiah who is Jesus Christ. He reprimanded those who had resisted the Holy Spirit and killed the Saviour, just as their forefathers had slaughtered the prophets whom God had sent to reveal His wishes for their benefit.

Saul and others from the Cilician synagogues who had come to Jerusalem to campaign against what sounded like blasphemy, were among those listening to Stephen. The crowd was so enraged by what they heard, and especially by his rebuke, that they took him outside the walls of the city and stoned this first Christian martyr to death. In this episode Saul is mentioned for the first time in the New Testament which records his approval of the stoning and that he even looked after the clothes of the executioners. It is not clear if the killing was the result of mob-frenzy which the leaders did nothing to restrain, or if it was ordered by the Sanhedrin who, because they did not have authority to pass a death sentence, took advantage of the interregnum between Pilate's recall to Rome and the arrival of his successor in AD 36. They then initiated a full-scale persecution of Christ's followers and appointed Saul their chief agent to eradicate the new movement from the synagogues and domestic life. Not satisfied with operating at a local level, he went north to Damascus to deal with those who had fled from persecution in Jerusalem but, like all dispersed Jews, were still under the jurisdiction of the Sanhedrin. (cf. *Ac* 7:1-60; 8:1-3; 22:5-20; *Ga* 2:1).

The Conversion of Saul

Armed with an escort and the written authority of the high
priest, Saul was within walking distance of Damascus
when a sudden burst of light flashed brighter than the sun
and he and his men fell to the ground. He heard a voice
asking him in Aramaic, "Why are you persecuting me? It
is hard to kick against the goad." Saul had always believed
he was acting in good faith but now the grace of God
began to work in him, enabling him to understand that in
persecuting the members of His Body he was persecuting
Jesus. The Pauline doctrine begins its life: Salvation
through faith and the grace of God, and Jesus is one with
His followers. A sense of divine intervention brought an
immediate and heartfelt obedience as he asked, "Who are
you Lord?" to be told, "I am Jesus and you are persecuting
me. Go now into the city and you will be told what you
have to do." By now the men had stood up, speechless,
hearing a voice but understanding nothing. When Paul, for
so we shall call him now, struggled to his feet he was
blind, and they had to lead him by the hand into the city
where for three days he could see nothing. When St Luke,
Paul's reliable companion and biographer, wrote the 'Acts
of the Apostles', he regarded this event of such
importance that he related it three times, once in his own
words and twice in those of Paul who was certain that the
appearance of Jesus at this miraculous meeting qualified
and gave him the privileges of an Apostle. Ananias who

was head of the community of believers in Damascus had misgivings about Paul but his mind was put at rest when Our Lord came to him in a vision and told him that this was the man He had chosen to bring His name before "pagans and pagan kings and before the people of Israel." He too, and Barnabas, later became convinced that the Lord had indeed been visible when speaking to Paul. The Fathers of the Church have commented upon the psychological preparation which accounts for the apparently instantaneous change of heart when he stopped kicking "against the goad", the prong which nudges oxen in the right direction. They believe that he had already been moved by the beauty of the Christian message and by Stephen's dying prayer for his killers, "Lord, do not hold this sin against them", which prompted St Augustine's comment, "If Stephen had not prayed, the Church would not have had Paul." (*Sermon* 315.)

Paul did not abandon his journey but entered Damascus with new purpose and fearless conviction. Ananias baptised and laid hands upon him so that he received the Holy Spirit and the restoration of his physical and spiritual sight. He had been blinded by the brilliance of Jesus' presence, but Baptism brought a clarity of vision and a determination to live and proclaim the Gospel of the crucified and risen Lord. The miraculous restoration of sight is the sign of the transformation of his life which continued to the end in an ever-increasing intensity of devotion because he felt he had more to expiate than most Apostles. His conversion is a manifestation of God's power to transform lives and we hear a similar life-long call to a change of heart, "to sing a new song to the Lord", which continues throughout life. (cf. *Ac* 9:1-19, 22:3-21, 26:9-19.)

Paul stayed in the house of one of the believers, a man called Judas, and there Jesus commissioned him to carry His name "first before pagans and pagan kings and then before the people of Israel." At this early stage he had already accepted that "Jesus was the only name in which there is salvation", and that mankind was saved through faith in Him who had been crucified in the name of the Old Law, the authority of which He now made effective. The revelation "I am Jesus and you are persecuting me", directs Paul's teaching that the faithful make up the Body of which Jesus is the Head, continuing the work of Redemption throughout time. (cf. *Ac* 9:15; *Ep* 4:16; *1 Co* 12:13ff.)

The new disciple then went to Arabia and, following the example of his Master, withdrew to a desert place to pray in preparation for his mission. He returned to Damascus about AD 35, and for the next three years preached the divine Sonship and Messianic character of Jesus in the synagogues. Some of the Jews branded him an apostate and plotted to kill him but the disciples helped him escape in a basket which they lowered down the city wall. He went to Jerusalem where he met Peter and James, but the community was understandably suspicious until Barnabas who was Mark's cousin and highly respected by the Apostles, vouched for him as "a good man" who had preached with great courage and success in Damascus. Our Lord appeared to him in the Temple and told him not to stay long in Jerusalem where the people would not believe the testimony about Him, and take the word to the pagans instead. Two weeks later, having seen no other Apostle, he went home to Tarsus which he made his base for the next four years. (*Ac* 4:26; 10:26-30, 22:17-21; *Ga* 1:17-19.)

The First Missionary Journey, AD 38-48

Peter had made the first evangelical contact with the Gentile world when he baptised the Roman centurion Cornelius, his family and household in Caesarea, though he had to justify his action to critical Jewish Christians when he returned to Jerusalem. Now, in Antioch-on-the-Orontes, not far from present-day Aleppo in Syria, refugee Christians were successfully preaching the Gospel, so the Apostles sent Barnabas to see if their efforts could benefit from support. First he collected Paul from Tarsus and the two went to Antioch which became such a vibrant centre of missionary activity that it was here that followers of Jesus were first officially recognised as "Christians". Its geographical position made it also an ideal place from which the Gospel could be taken to Asia Minor and Greece.

From Antioch, Paul and Barnabus sailed to Cyprus, Barnabas' birthplace, and then on to Perga in south-west Turkey, calling at another Antioch in Pisidia, Iconium, Lystra, and Derbe. More often than not they opened their missions in the synagogues, but it was the non-Jews who responded to their preaching and miracles with most enthusiasm. Paul, who had quickly assumed leadership and was conscious of the Jews' resistance to the Gospel, said to them, "We had to proclaim the word of God to you first, but since you have rejected it, since you do not think yourselves worthy of eternal life, we must turn to the pagans". Some Jewish opposition was so violent that at Lystra, for example, Paul was stoned and left for dead, but he and Barnabas bravely returned along the route they had come, encouraging and organising new groups of believers to whom they would later return to appoint priests in each church and consolidate progress. (cf. *Ac* 13, 14.)

In AD 48, they accompanied a delegation from Antioch to discuss the status of Gentile Christians with the leaders of the Church in Jerusalem. Some Judaeans were insistant that salvation was not possible without circumcision according to the Law which God had given to Moses, and for Paul this raised a question of policy as well as principle. To accept such teaching would negate his mission to the Gentiles, dash his hopes of "gaining the world for Christ", and be a denial of the intrinsic merits of His Sacrifice on the Cross and His death which opens the way to salvation. To impose national or racial regulations on converts was contrary to his certainty that Christ died for all without distinction. Eventually, the Apostles recognised his membership of the Apostolic College and approved his mission to the Gentiles, support which he found reassuring and most timely in view of the bitter hostility he was encountering from many Jewish Christians. Peter, supported by James, proposed the freedom of Gentile Christians and it was agreed that, unlike their Jewish counterparts, they were not obliged to be circumcised or be subject to Mosaic law. When the leaders in Jerusalem sent Paul and Barnabas back to Antioch with their decision, one of their number, a Roman citizen called Silas or "Silvanus", went with them. Paul found him very much a kindred spirit and, for reasons which will be explained later, chose him rather than Barnabas as the companion for his next mission. (cf. *Ac* 15.)

The Second and Third Missionary Journeys, AD 49-58

The second and third journeys which started from and ended in Jerusalem are referred to as the "Aegean Mission" because this region saw eight years of sustained activity. He and Silas travelled through Syria, Cilicia and the Galatian towns which had been evangelised during the first mission. When they were refused entry to Bithynia in the north, they turned west past Mysia to Troas on the coast and, in answer to an appeal they received in a vision, they continued on to Philippi in the

Roman province of Macedonia where they were joined by Luke and Timothy. The city, named after Philip II of Macedon, enjoyed colony status which had been granted by Mark Antony and Octavian after defeating Brutus and Cassius in 42 BC, governed itself according to imperial law, and was exempt from poll and land taxes.

Here the mission began favourably with the conversion of Lydia, a lady who was a successful cloth-merchant from Thyatira. Then they freed a slave girl who was a fortune-teller from a troublesome spirit, but her masters were furious that the exorcism and her new-found faith deprived them of the income from her sooth-saying. They complained to the magistrates that Paul and Silas were creating a disturbance contrary to Roman law, with the result that they were beaten and thrown into gaol, the first instance of persecution not initiated by the Jews. The exorcism may have been interpreted maliciously as a public religious challenge to the prophetic powers attributed to the Greek god Apollo, or even to the worship of the emperor as a divinity, but the incarceration was not to be lengthy. One night, as the two prisoners were praying and singing God's praises, a sudden earthquake flung open the doors and burst their chains, a miracle which inspired the gaoler's confession of belief and the baptism of his household.

When the magistrates discovered that the prisoners were Roman citizens, they feared repercussions and released them immediately on condition that they left the city immediately. Paul and Barnabus went to Thessalonika, the capital of Macedonia, where they preached successfully until some Jewish antipathy forced them to flee to Berea. They stopped briefly at Athens where Paul soon recovered from the disappointment and, with enthusiastic energy restored, they made for Corinth on the maritime route between Rome and the East, which was to be the centre of Paul's activity for the next eighteen months. He earned his living as a tent-maker so that he should not be a burden on the church in Corinth, and because he wanted to distinguish himself from those wandering philosophers and politicians who expected free board and lodging. When opposition from the synagogue again made life difficult, Our Lord came in another vision to tell him to move on to a more fruitful Gentile field and assured him, "Do not be afraid to speak out, nor allow yourself to be silenced. I am with you and no one will ever attempt to hurt you."

Paul returned briefly to Antioch before setting out on the third major journey which took him through Galacia, Phrygia, and then to Ephesus, the flourishing capital of the Roman province of Asia. He preached persuasively in the synagogue about the Kingdom of God, and for three months all went well until some of the congregation began to attack his teaching. He moved to the lecture rooms in the school of Tyrranus where he led daily discussions for two years, and Jews and Gentiles alike came from all over Asia to hear the word of the Lord. The number of converts grew, the Gospel was carried to the Lycus valley, and Christian groups were formed in the cities of Colossae, Laodicia and Hierapolis. That his time in Ephesus was not without problems is evident when he writes to the Corinthians about the many adversaries he had there, of being in constant danger, and fighting with "wild beasts", no doubt a metaphor for the savagery of the opposition with which he had to contend. (cf. *Ac* 16-20; *1 Cor* 16:8-9.)

The Final Years

With the Church in Ephesus firmly established and the evangelisation of the east ended for the time being, Paul decided to take the news of Christ to the far west where it had not yet reached. The Gentile Christians had collected alms for the poor of the Mother-church as proof of their loyalty and their communion in the family of believers, so he decided to take their donation to Jerusalem via Macedonia and Arabia, and then continue on to Rome. He had no doubts about the fate which eventually awaited him, and his farewell speech to the Ephesian elders has been called his last will and testament. It reveals a timeless nobility, heroism, and selfless dedication to Christ and His work of Redemption.

"You can witness how I have lived among you since I came to Asia, humbly serving the Lord, not without tears over the trials I endured when the Jews plotted against me, and how I have never failed you when there was a need for preaching or teaching either in public places or in your own homes. To both Jew and Gentile I have proclaimed repentance before God, and faith in Our Lord Jesus Christ. As far as I can see, I am already a prisoner but I am going to Jerusalem even though I do not know what is going to happen to me and, as I go from city to city, the Holy Spirit warns me that only prison and suffering awaits me there. That does not concern me because my life is of less value than my responsibility to preach as the Lord Jesus directs, proclaiming the good news of God's grace. I am well aware that I came and returned to you preaching the Kingdom of God, and that you will not see me again but you know today that I am innocent of any person's blood and have never hesitated to tell you the whole of God's plan. Keep careful watch over God's Church in which the Holy Spirit has appointed you bishops to be shepherds of the Flock which He has won for Himself by shedding His Blood. I am sure that, when I have gone, hungry wolves will descend on the flock and will not spare it. Some will come from your own ranks and attract followers with their false message. Be on your guard and remember the three years I spent teaching every one of you until I was weeping. As I did then, I now commend you to God and His gracious promise which will sustain you and give you your inheritance among all those whom He has made holy. You know that I have never asked for money or clothes and that I worked to keep myself and my companions. I have always tried to show you that we have a duty to work and support the vulnerable remembering Our Lord's own words, 'It is more blessed to give than to receive'. When he had finished, he knelt and prayed with them, and by now they were all in tears. They put their arms around Paul and kissed him, heartbroken that they should never see him again, and kept him company as far as his ship." (cf. *Ac* 19:21-31, 20:18-38, tr. JBM; *Rm* 15:19.)

A Prisoner for Christ

Paul had not been long in Jerusalem when some Asian Jews who were on pilgrimage for the feast of Pentecost accused him of violating the Temple by entering with a number of Greek Gentiles. A riot ensued during which he would have been beaten to death had it not been for the intervention of the Roman tribune commanding the garrison who took him into protective custody. When he declared his Roman citizenship he was allowed to address the crowd, but the rioters shouted him down. He was then transferred to the Fortress Antonia, the military base named after Mark Antony, which offered a vantage point overlooking the Temple precincts and enabled early recognition and suppression of the frequent disturbances.

That night "the Lord appeared to Paul and said, 'Courage! You have born witness for me in Jerusalem; now you must do the same in Rome.'" In the morning the tribune intended to bring Paul before the Sanhedrin, but when he discovered that forty men had vowed to fast until they had killed him, he sent him under guard to Felix, the Governor stationed in Caesarea who, merely to avoid further trouble, unjustly imprisoned him from AD 57-59. When Festus succeeded Felix, the Jewish leaders tried to have Paul brought to trial in Jerusalem but he invoked his right as a Roman citizen to be tried before the emperor, and so by-passed the Governor's jurisdiction. In the first instance, he presented his case before Herod Agrippa II in a speech of impressive moderation, prudence, and respect for his hearers and the Law. (cf. *Ac* 21; 17-24:26, 26.)

In autumn AD 60, Paul and other prisoners were put on board a ship sailing to Rome but they were shipwrecked off the coast of Malta. This was his fourth such perilous experience, but the Lord had assured him in a vision that all the passengers would be saved, and so it proved. They spent the winter months on the island and, on one occasion, Paul was bitten by a snake as he was collecting firewood. Since he was unharmed, he was regarded as something of a god, an opinion further strengthened when he healed the father of Publius, the Prefect of the island. Others were brought to him to be cured and, by the time he boarded another ship three months later, he had won the veneration of the Maltese people. Accompanied by Luke, he landed at Puteoli and from there went on foot to Rome where Christians came out to welcome him at the Appian Market and escort him on the final stage which some have likened to his Master's Way of the Cross.

For two years Paul was under house-arrest in his own rented accommodation, but this did not slow the progress of the Gospel even as far as the Praetorian Guard who lodged with him, and the imperial palace itself. "He welcomed all who came to visit him, proclaiming the Kingdom of God and teaching the truth about the Lord Jesus with complete freedom and without hindrance from anyone." (*Ac* 28:30-31.) The Four "Captivity" Letters show his determination not to allow circumstances to hinder his teaching. From the fullness of his heart he writes to his beloved Philippians about the peace and spiritual joy he experiences and which he wants them, his children, to share. In his letter to the Ephesians he celebrates the eternal love of the Holy Trinity which is poured out for the salvation of mankind, the triumphant supremacy of Christ, and the abundance of grace which flows from Him to His body which is the Church. To the Colossians he explains Christ's pre-eminence, and warns them against the plausible arguments with which some inhabitants of the Lycus valley might try to adapt the Faith to their own philosophy. The Letter to Philemon,

the only one addressed to a private individual about a
personal matter, reveals the wrtiter's warmth, charm, and
attitude to social and political evil.

Release and Last Journey

St Clement (d. AD 101) in his Epistle (5:5-7) and St John
Chrysostom (349-407) both attest that, after his release,
Paul ventured as far west as Spain, and the Letters
mention some of the stopping places on his last
missionary journey eastward. At Crete he left Titus to
correct any errors that still persisted, and he entrusted
Ephesus to Timothy's benevolent supervision. He wrote
to them from Macedonia urging them to be good
ministers for Jesus Christ, to encourage sound doctrine,
and persuade those who dissented to a better frame of
mind. He spent the winter in Nicopolis where he was
joined by Titus en route to Dalmatia after his successful
mission in Crete, before making quick visits to Troas,
Miletus and Corinth. As soon as he arrived back in Rome
he was arrested again, but this time the earlier, civilised
custody was replaced by a confinement where he was
virtually incommunicado.

The atmosphere in Rome had changed and Christians
were under siege with only their faith to sustain them.
Paul's last letter to his dear friend Timothy begged him to
come quickly for he was expecting the end, though with
confidence unshaken. "All there is to come now is the

crown of righteousness reserved for me, which the Lord, the righteous judge, will give to me on that day, and not only to me but to all those who have longed for his coming." (*2 Tim* 4:8.) Like Peter, Paul was a victim of Nero's persecution and was beheaded at Aquae Salviae a few miles outside the walls of Rome on the Ostia road, and was buried by his friends in a cemetery some way towards the city. In the fourth century Constantine built the great Basilica of 'Saint Paul outside the Walls' where the Apostle and Martyr lay. The Epistle which Pope Saint Clement (d. 101) sent to the Corinthians gives evidence of the residence, co-operation, and martyrdom in Rome of both Peter and Paul.

THOSE WHO WORKED WITH PAUL

Paul chose his collaborators with great care, and it seems that loyalty to him and his methods were prime considerations. His positive leadership was not always palatable but under his tuition they profited from his intellect and the example of his tireless dedication to became splendid lieutenants able to complement, continue and extend his work. Those who had been personal followers of Jesus, or converted to Christianity before they attached themselves to Paul, demonstrate that he was always of one mind in faith with the Apostles.

Luke

The author of the third Gospel and the 'Acts of the Apostles' was a Greek physician whom some say had been a personal follower of Our Lord and one of the two disciples to whom He revealed Himself in the breaking of bread at Emmaus in the evening of the Day of Resurrection. (cf. *Lk* 24:13-35.) Certainly he was a pioneer of the Christian community at Antioch and became Paul's disciple and the close companion. He was his leader's faithful diarist, shielded him from criticism, recorded his apostolate with care and admiration, and earned from him the tributes "fellow-worker" and "beloved physician".

His writings which are similar in style and subject, reveal literary flair, sensitivity, and facility in Hellenist rhetoric. His Gospel written with a Gentile audience in mind, includes the account of the Virgin birth of the world's Saviour, and emphasises the comfort of divine compassion in the moving parables of the Good Samaritan and the Prodigal Son, Our Lord's gentle words to the women of Jerusalem as He struggled with the Cross to Calvary, and His beatific promise to the repentant thief crucified next to Him. It is his Gospel which most honours women in the persons of the Blessed Virgin Mary who is the Mother of God, Elizabeth her cousin and mother of John the Baptist, the widow of Nairn, and Mary Magdalen. In the 'Acts' he links sacred and secular history, and traces the progression of Christianity from Jerusalem into the Gentile world, especially the heart of the Roman empire. Tradition has it that, like Paul, he was celibate all his life and died in Boetia at the age of eighty-four. Not surprisingly, doctors and surgeons have adopted him as their patron, and so too have artists because of the word-pictures he draws so beautifully. Flemish painters of the fifteenth and sixteenth centuries have depicted him painting an icon of the Blessed Virgin and his symbol is an ox, presumably because his Gospel opens with reference to the Temple sacrifice. The Feast-day of Saint Luke, Evangelist, is October 18th.

Barnabas

We know that when Paul arrived in Jerusalem and tried to join the disciples, their leaders doubted that anyone with his fearsome reputation for persecution could be trusted. Barnabas, whose Hebrew name means "son of consolation", was a Levite from Cyprus who had been one of Our Lord's followers. He had donated the proceeds from the sale of his property to the infant Christian community and was highly regarded by the Apostles. He vouched for Paul and told them all how boldly and persuasively he had preached in Damascus in the name of the Lord. He became his collaborator in Antioch, the companion of the first missionary journey, and together they attended the apostolic council of Jerusalem which settled the vexed question of whether or not the Gentile Christians' were subject to circumcision and the Mosaic Law.

Barnabas wanted John Mark to accompany them on the second missionary journey but, as we shall see in a moment, Paul disagreed, and there was a further difference of opinion about the appropriate form of table-fellowship between Jewish and Gentile Christians. Though this led to a parting of their ways, Paul always praised him as a model of apostolic endeavour. Barnabas went with Mark back to Cyprus where he established the Church and, according to Tertullian and others, contributed to the letter to the Hebrews. He gave his life

for the Faith when he was stoned to death at Salamis
about AD 61. The Feast of Saint Barnabas, Apostle, is
June 11th and he is among the Saints invoked in the
Roman Canon of the Mass. (cf. *Ac* 4:36-7, 9:27, 11:22-
30, 13-15, *1 Co* 9:6; *Ga* 2:1-14.)

Mark

John Mark, whose mother Mary owned a house in
Jerusalem where the early Christians gathered, was a
cousin of Barnabas and is best known as the author of the
second Gospel. Paul and Barnabas delivered alms for the
relief of the poor who were suffering from the famine, and
when they returned to Antioch they took Mark with them.
He helped them proclaim the Gospel in Cyprus but, for
some reason, he did not continue with them to Turkey,
returning instead to Jerusalem much to Paul's
disappointment. When the second missionary journey was
being planned in Antioch and Barnabas suggested that
they take Mark with them, Paul refused because he had
not completed the first journey. He chose Silas to
accompany him to Syria, Cilicia and Macedonia, while
Barnabas and Mark went back to Cyprus.

There seems to have been no animosity, for Paul, in the
letter to Philemon, speaks of Mark as one of his collaborators,
asks the Colossians to receive him hospitably, and in his
second letter to Timothy expresses warm appreciation of the
value of his contribution. Mark was later in Rome with Peter

who refers to him affectionately as his "son" in the faith, and provided him with material for his Gospel. Eusebius tells us that Mark took Christianity to Egypt and founded the church in Alexandria where he was the first bishop. According to tradition, he was martyred during the latter part of Nero's reign, and in the ninth century his relics were brought to Venice, of which city he is the patron saint. The Feast of Saint Mark, Evangelist is celebrated on April 25th. (cf. *Ac* 11:27-30, 12:12-25, 13:13; *1 P* 5:13; *Eccl. Hist.* 20. 16:1-2; 2:24.)

Silas

Silvanus was a colleague of Paul and Timothy, and shared with Paul the double privilege of Jewish blood and Roman citizenship. He was chosen to take the letter from the Council in Jerusalem to the Christians in Antioch and was Paul's preferred companion on the second missionary journey. He contributed to the two letters to the Thessalonians and was the scribe for Peter's first letter. It is believed that he died in Macedonia. In the West the Feast of Saint Silas is celebrated on July 13th and, in the Orthodox churches which number him among the bishops of Corinth, on June 30th or November 26th.

Apollos

Apollos was a Jew from Alexandria who had been converted by Aquila and Priscilla. He was Paul's trusted friend and worked with him in Corinth where his eloquence in the rhetoric popular in the Hellenist provinces appealed to those who had benefited from a more privileged education. Paul warned them that this was no reason to consider themselves superior to others because eloquence is not as important as the value of the Christian message and its demonstration of the power of the Holy Spirit. (cf. *Ac* 18:24-28; *1 Co* 2:4.)

Timothy and Titus

Timothy was born in Lystra, the son of a Jewish mother and Gentile father. He was converted by Paul during the first missionary journey, with mother Eunice and his grandmother Lois. He became a trusted collaborator on the third missionary journey, often going ahead of his leader and staying behind to consolidate after he left. Paul had every confidence in his warm-hearted friend who, despite a natural reserve, successfully handled delicate assignments in Thessalonika, Ephesus, Corinth, and Philippi. He looked on him as a son, described him as his "beloved and faithful child", and included him in the greeting to the recipients of five letters. Timothy shared Paul's first Roman captivity and went with him on the last visit to Ephesus where he later became the first bishop. From the apocryphal 'Acts of Timothy' we learn that he was martyred because of his opposition to pagan festivals which were organised in honour of Dionysius.

Titus, a Gentile from Antioch-on-the-Orontes, was converted by Paul who refers to him as "my beloved son". He went with Paul and Barnabas to the Council of Jerusalem during which Paul resisted calls for his circumcision. He accompanied the Apostle on the third missionary journey, and his reliability and willingness to undertake any kind of work were invaluable. Paul sent him on urgent and sensitive missions to Corinth where he restored harmony by settling the dispute that had arisen between his leader and the church there. Paul delegated to him the organisation of the church in Crete where he is honoured as the first bishop. Saints Timothy and Titus share the same feast-day on January 26th appropriately the day after the Feast of the Conversion of Saint Paul. (cf. *1 Co* 4:17, 16:10-11; *1 Tm* 1:3-4; *Tt* 1:4-5; *Ga* 2.)

The "churches"

Throughout the 'Acts of the Apostles' and Paul's letters, reference is made to the "church" in, for example, Ephesus, Corinth, or Rome and, at this point, some recollection of background, architecture, and dedicated membership may be useful. The concept of house and home was very dear to the Roman empire and when Christianity with its developing liturgy began to flourish, it was natural that there should be a move from the Judaeic synagogue to the household. This had the added advantage of warding off the attention of the authorities who were inclined to wonder if religious sects and group gatherings were planning to sow seeds of rebellion. In times of persecution survival depended on discretion and the "house-church" appeared no more suspect than a group from the synagogue meeting as guests of the host to have a meal, study the scriptures, and reflect upon Our Lord's words and deeds.

At the Last Supper on the night before He died, Our Lord "broke bread" according to the Jewish rite of giving thanks for food. The disciples honoured His injunction to celebrate the Eucharist and, in the early days, did so at a meal. They also continued to worship in the synagogue and in the Temple because, although Jesus had foretold its destruction, it was still His Father's house. When Christianity was established in places at a distance like Antioch, the faithful assembled in private homes for the Breaking of Bread and praising the Lord. When doing so, they preserved aspects of the Temple's liturgy like praying at the third, sixth and ninth hours, and at the time appointed for the evening sacrifice.

Where numbers made the existence of a synagogue viable, it remained the ideal place to introduce the Gospel to the Jews and those Gentiles who had attached themselves to the community, perhaps because they were initially contemplating conversion to Judaeism. The private home, however, was more convenient for the distinctive Eucharistic liturgy, and the assembly of house groups constituted the first "churches". Even affluent homes were relatively modest in size, so the groups must have been fairly small, perhaps twenty to fifty at most. Paul, always sensitive to human tendencies, insisted that whenever the group assembled as a church to share a meal as a memorial of the Lord's Eucharist, their behaviour should be beyond reproach, and there should be no argument. (cf. *Ac* 2:46, 12:12-17, 18:7, 20:7-12; *Rm* 16:23; *1 Co* 10:16, 11:18, 14:26-31; *Col* 4:15.)

THEMES OF SAINT PAUL'S LETTERS

The New Testament lists Paul's letters in an order of diminishing length which opens with Romans until concluding with Hebrews. The order in which they were written, however, shows the development of his theological thought as he articulates the depth and meaning of the Gospel. The early Church is dealing with problems not confined to any particular place or time, like internal rivalries, external temptations and distractions, disloyal members, liturgical abuse, idolatry of one kind or another, accommodating the spirit of the age, teaching false doctrine, in fact the sort of hellish, though futile, assaults which Christ foretold would be made on His Church. With a marvellous fusion of straight-speaking and tenderness which St John Chrysostom describes as his characteristic "trumpet notes", Paul deals with circumstances as he finds them and offers the universal solution in the contemplation of Christ with whom the soul is united. He has a clear vision of the universal efficacy of Redemption by Christ in whom there is neither Jew nor Gentile, and the salvation which comes through faith in Him "who was put to death for our sins and raised to life to justify us." The Law of Moses, on the other hand, though it was holy and just could not save or help those engaged in the battle against sin and death.

The supremacy of the life of grace over external observance frees Christians from the Mosaic Law, though they are still subject to the law of the Spirit. By His death, Christ delivered the human race from the tyranny of sin and death, and the Christian, now united with the Risen Christ in a new life, can give the joyous service which the Holy Spirit inspires. The "slaves of Christ" are truly at liberty because "where the spirit of the Lord is there is freedom." (*Rm* 4:25; *2 Co* 3:17.)

When Paul was baptised by Ananias and his sight restored after the blinding experience on the Damascus road, he had eyes only for Jesus, and the assumed title in which he most rejoiced was "Slave of Jesus Christ". He was spurred on by faith in the crucified Lord "in whom we gain our freedom, the forgiveness of our sins. He is the image of the unseen God and the first born of all creation, for in Him were created all things in heaven and on earth... Before anything was created He existed, and He holds all things in unity. And He is head of the Body, the Church, and the beginning and first-born from the dead. In all things He takes primacy because God wanted all perfection to be found in him, and everything to be reconciled to Himself through Him who makes peace by His death on the Cross." (*Col* 1:14-20.)

Christ is the object of Paul's constant love and heartfelt praise, and nothing is going to separate him from that love, not even hunger, nakedness, suffering and persecution. For him life is Christ and death a wonderful triumph. Because he has been crucified with Christ, he does not live his own life now, but the life of Christ who lives in him, and no one on earth can disturb him because he carries on his body the marks of Christ. The phrase "in Christ Jesus" is a favourite acknowledgement which permeates his thoughts as he writes, and his ardent love for his Lord shines across the centuries. From a dark dungeon he sees the Saviour's light shining rays of immortal life through the Gospel he has been appointed to preach. Any painful memories in the service of the Lord give way to the consolation of God's peace which fills hearts and minds in Christ Jesus. "The Lord has rescued me from every evil attempt upon me and brings me safely to His Heavenly Kingdom. To Him be glory for ever and ever. Amen." (Cf. *Rm* 8:35; *Ph* 1:21; *Ga* 2:19-20, 6:14-17; *1 Tm* 1:10; *2 Tm* 4:18.)

As a Jew, Paul believed in the one true and living God who reveals Himself in the Scriptures, is active in the world in His choice of the people of Israel, and is faithful to the promises He made to the Patriarchs which are find completed in Christ. (cf. *Rm* 15:8.) His experience on the road to Damascus brought understanding of the life, death and Resurrection of Christ the the Son of God, eternal before time and the Incarnation, equal to the Father in His divinity and entitled to the same worship. In Him, God rescues His people from a situation in which they are powerless to help themselves. Life and death are transformed, the Old Law is sublimated in a New Covenant, and the work of redemption and sanctification is accomplished. After His Resurrection from the dead and Ascension into Heaven, Jesus Christ who is God and Man sits in equality at the Father's right hand, and unites human nature to the Holy Trinity.

Salvation

In the story of Adam, Paul observes how human nature, invaded by sin and death, has become wounded and frail. He sees Christ as the New Adam who frees us, and he expresses this liberation in the metaphors of slaves being ransomed, debts cancelled, and charges being dismissed in a court of law. The shedding of the Precious Blood which characterises the Passion and the establishment of the New Covenant, brings victory over the powers of evil, removes the divisions in humanity, and transforms death to life in the Risen Christ who is "Lord of the living and the dead". To be "in Christ", is to share His death and Resurrection in Baptism. It is the new life which Paul experiences himself and longs to share with his readers through the Holy Spirit, the sign and confirmation of the new creation who endows all believers with His gifts and graces. (cf. *1 Co* 12:1-11; *2 Co* 5:16-21; *Ga* 3:28, 5:13-26; *Rm* 5-6, 8:28-39, 14:7-9.)

The Church

The Church is the Mystical Body of Christ who makes no distinction between Jew and Gentile, and saves all through faith in Him rather than through observance of the Mosaic Law. Everyone who believes in Him will share the glory of the final Resurrection at the end of time when He presents the perfected Kingdom to His Father. The gifts which the Holy Spirit bestows on individuals are not so that they can compete with one another, but so that they can co-operate in the Mystical Body, like the limbs and organs which compose the physical body. God enables us to lead a life which is directed by love for Him, and He compensates for human failure, inspires repentance and, steadfast in compassion, is always ready to forgive. In Christ He triumphs over sin and death once and for all and, in return, asks only that we believe and acknowledge Him with grateful trust. In Baptism, the Mystical Body shares the victory and a new life enhanced by the gifts of the Holy Spirit begins.

Paul sees "church" as more than building, an ecclesiastical organisation, or a denomination. It is the community of all joined together in Christ, and wherever there is a body of believers. In Thessalonika, for example, every member has a special place and function to serve and help others as do the limbs and organs of the physical body. When he wanted to send a message to a church, he usually dictated it to one of his aides like Timothy or

Silas. They were not intended as polished literary compositions and he had no idea that they would be studied throughout time, and extracts read in the universal Christian Church today. The style can be sometimes be jerky, even obscure, though Paul delights in repetition so that important points are emphasised in different ways, but minor blemishes do not affect the sublimity of thought and grandeur of expression. He recommends that God's word in Scripture is allowed to influence discipleship and the vocation of being servants of Christ, the stewards of God's mysteries who are entrusted with guarding the deposit of faith. We must not be discouraged by a fear of failure to live up to God's expectations for He is with us in all that He wants us to do, giving us His Spirit to guide us, and His Church through which He gives us the Sacraments of His grace to sustain us on our way. (cf, *1 Co* 4:1-5, 12:12-31; *Ga* 3, 6:8; *Rm* 6:1-10, 8; *Ep* 2:13-16, 4:1-16.)

1 AND 2 THESSALONIANS AD 50-51

Paul and Silas travelled along the Egyptian way from Philippi to Thessalonika, then the chief naval station of the Macedonian kingdom and now Salonika in Greece. The population was mainly Greek but, because of the city's prosperity, there was an influential Jewish community with its own synagogue where they preached the Gospel for a few weeks. Some Jews accepted the message but others, not for the only time, stirred up resentment against the two missioners who had to make a hasty departure. Paul is now writing from Corinth during his second missionary journey and his subject is the pursuit of holiness in preparation for Christ's coming. With the church in Thessalonika he rejoices in the Holy Spirit that they have embraced the Gospel despite the surrounding opposition, and that the converts have abandoned idolatry "and become servants of the real living God." He longed to see them again but circumstances prevented his return, "Satan blocked our way", so he sent Timothy from Athens to support future progress. Timothy made two visits before he returned to Corinth and gave a glowing report to Paul who wrote to the Thessalonians to say how happy he was that the faith had not only survived but was flourishing. He encourages good behaviour, the development of a vibrant and harmonious Christian community, and the avoidance of the sexual immorality which he knew often characterised city-ports. He advises them to "attend to your own business, earning your living so that you are seen to be respectable by those outside the Church."

The early Christians expected to be alive at the time of the "Parousia", Our Lord's Second Coming on the last day, and wondered what would happen to those who had already died. Paul assures them that they will not be at a disadvantage when Jesus returns in glory because, like Him, they will be raised from the dead and, with those who are still alive, be with Him forever. In that supreme moment, "corruptible bodies will put on incorruption" and death will finally have lost all its power. That the Parousia was expected at any time is shown in the expectant prayer "Maran Atha", "Come Lord", and in Paul's advice to remain in one's present state and to lead an upright life so as not to be taken by surprise, because "our time is short... May you all be kept safe and blameless, spirit, soul and body, for the coming of Our Lord Jesus Christ." This harmonises with the Gospel, the teaching of the Church today, and with what he said at the Council of the Areopagus in Athens, "God tells everyone, everywhere that they must repent because He has fixed a day when the whole world will be judged in righteousness." He adds that it is sensible to keep to life's daily routine and earn a living, rather than stand around gossiping like those who were just waiting for the end. When Constantine became emperor in the fourth century, his sympathy for Christianity encouraged an emphasis on the Church's historic success and progress. As the resultant confidence grew, expectations of an imminent Parousia faded but, as the early Creeds and statements of belief demonstrate, the certainty of Jesus' eventual return as the Heavenly Judge remained undiminished. (cf. *Ac* 17:1-9, 31; *1 Th* 1:6, 9, 4:12-18; *1 Co* 7:25-31, 15:23; *2 P* 1:16, 3:4; *Mt* 24: 3-41.)

1 AND 2 CORINTHIANS AD 57

Corinth, a few miles south-west of the narrow stretch of
land which joined north and south Greece, was the capital
of the province of Achaia and strategically positioned to
enjoy commercial advantages. Cargoes and even small
ships bound east or west in the Mediterranean landed on
one side of the isthmus, were carried across to the other
and then reloaded for departure. The Isthmian Games held
every two years also contributed to the healthy economy
by drawing crowds larger than those which attended the
Olympics. The many Jews who had settled here justified
the establishment of more than one synagogue, but they
were not given Corinthian citizenship nor were they
popular in a city steeped in Roman tradition. As a sea-port
it attracted a variety of philosophies and religions but the
moral tone of public behaviour left much to be desired,
and converts to Christianity needed supportive guidance in
the way of life recommended by the Gospel.

Paul, accompanied by Silas and Timothy, first arrived
to preach the Gospel in Corinth about AD 49 and stayed
for eighteen months. His converts included a number of
Jews but the majority were Gentile artisans, freedmen,
servants and slaves. When he left in AD 51, Apollos
carried on his work, and the faithful had increased in
number before he rejoined him at Ephesus. A year-long

visit from some Palestinian Christians exemplifies the problems experienced by the early Church in the major cities of the Roman world, and the enormity of Paul's task which was made more difficult by the very people from whom he was entitled to expect support. The "false prophets", as he calls them, undermined his work, contradicted his teaching, tolerated laxity, and generally undermined the spiritual life. Some of the converts who considered themselves better educated and more enlightened, succumbed to their influence and claimed superior insights into religious observance. They adopted a liberal attitude towards immoral behaviour and idolatrous practices, and ridiculed the orthodoxy of others. The latter were so anxious that three of their leaders travelled to Ephesus with a letter to Paul urging him to come to Corinth and save the situation. He decided to postpone a confrontation with the troublemakers and, instead, wrote to the community so that they could have an opportunity to reflect on matters of principle rather than on personal issues. From 1 and 2 Corinthians, however, a sequence of additional correspondence is apparent in an early letter from Paul, (cf. *1 Co* 7:1); a further letter of which no notice was taken, (cf. *1 Co* 5:9); the 'First Letter' answering the questions posed by the Corinthians; an anguished letter from Paul which they found painful, (cf. *2 Co* 2:4); the 'Second Letter' intended to restore good relations and mutual understanding.

The First Letter

After clarifying his apostolic role and authority, Paul attends to the problems associated with the lax attitude to immoral behaviour, internal factions and disputes, pagan socialising, liberal views on sex and marriage, and an irreverent party-spirit during the Lord's Supper. He asserts his right and responsibility as Christ's Apostle and founder of the church in Corinth to correct faults and misunderstandings, and eloquently expresses his heartfelt desire to win over the waverers. He says that true wisdom and knowledge are not found in human pride but in the humility of the despised and crucified Saviour who lights the way to love and the life of the Spirit. He reprimands the unrepentant, those who take their disputes to the civil court rather than have them resolved in the church community, and those who eat the food which has been prepared for the idolatrous festivals. He uses the Scriptures familiar to the Jews, Christ's teaching, and his own theology to promote the Christian way of life.

He reminds the faithful of their duty of obedience to state government as a precept of God's moral law, and then makes his incomparable exhortation to Charity. In the New Testament, the word used for "love" is the Greek "agape" which emanates from the "great commandment" to love God, one's neighbours, and even one's enemies. Paul, understands "agape" as the hallmark of Christian life in the evolvement of God's plan of salvation through Christ and the Spirit of Truth, and it outshines even faith and hope. The word became associated with a special meal or "love-feast" in which divine and human love are manifest in a shared communion and fellowship. Little distinction was made between community meals and the Eucharist, which is the Sacrament of the Lord's love, the institution of which is beautifully remembered in the letter. The sublimely precise consideration of charity has a wonderful coherence with the Gospels and the letters of St John, revealing again the Holy Spirit at work in the Scriptures.

After the commandment to love and worship God, charity is the first rule of conduct towards human beings. He who loves his neighbour will be anxious not to do him wrong and where there is such loving-kindness, all other commandments will be observed as a matter of course. Love is more a decision than an emotion, a determination to make the well-being of others the motivation for action, an outpouring of life in service so that the whole of humanity becomes a sacrifice acceptable to the Father. Paul combines principle and realism when he advocates celibacy as a way of life which enlarges freedom to serve God, but he recognises that it is not an option for many, and that a physical relationship is part of married life.

There is guidance for the proper conduct of the Liturgy and appropriate behaviour during worship. Paul makes it clear that an appreciation of the mystery of the Eucharist embraces a sensitive consideration for others in the Body

of Christ whose individual ministries and gifts from God
are interdependent. He assumes that a belief in the Real
Presence will inspire sensitivity to others and the greatest
reverence in the Eucharistic celebration, and skilfully
combines bluntness with persuasion to attract others to his
point of view. He presents the earliest written evidence of
Christ's Resurrection as the model and guarantee of the
bodily resurrection in which all will share when He comes
again, but with a transformed body which is glorious and
immortal. Finally, he explains the arrangements for the
collection of contributions to help the mother-church in
Jerusalem, his travel plans, and concludes typically, "My
love is with you all in Christ Jesus." To follow up the
effects of the letter, he sent Titus to Corinth and he was
able to report back that loyalty and reverence had been
rekindled. (cf. *Rm* 5:5, 9:13-15, 13:10; *1 Co* 10:1, 11:17-
34, 13:1-13; *1 Jn* 4:8-16; *Mt* 5:43, 22:39-40, 24:12; *Mk*
12:28; *Lk* 11:42; *Jn* 13:35, 15:9-13.)

The Second Letter

Paul is comforted by Titus' report that he now had the
support of the majority of the Christians in Corinth, and he
expresses his happiness that reconciliation has been
reached after a disagreement which had caused him so
much anxiety. Now he speaks of the unity of the Church,
the role of the apostolate, and the conditions that make for
the fruitful exercise of that responsibility. There are details

about the crisis and his earlier life, but it is as a spiritual guide that the letter is most important. When he speaks of the efficacy which union with Christ brings to suffering, he is thinking particularly of the burdens which beset a true disciple and which are the foundation of the pursuit of holiness. The harsh inevitability of suffering is softened by Paul's joyful hope of immortality and the tender affection which shines through the statements of reconciliation.

There are further references to the collection for the Jerusalem community and, towards the end, Paul again denounces "false apostles". He issues a last warning to rebels, rebuts slanders, appeals to the obstinate, promises a further visit, wishes everyone happiness, love, and the peace of God, and asks them all to "greet one another with the holy kiss." Later, when he visited Corinth and spent a few months there, he may have excommunicated some who refused to comply but, generally speaking, an atmosphere of purposeful faith was restored. Throughout, he has celebrated the supernatural character of Christianity which is founded on divine wisdom and power. Other passages contributing to a treasury of spiritual devotion consider the wisdom of the Cross (*2 Co* 1:18-2:8), the self-renunciation which is required of the Apostle (2 Co 4:9ff), the fundamental basis of marital and celibate chastity (*2 Co* 6:15-20), detachment from the world (*2 Co* 7:29-32), and consideration for others (*2 Co* 8:11-13).

GALATIANS, ROMANS AD 57-58

Galatia was the name the Romans gave to the province in northern Asia Minor. Paul is writing to the church, in what is now Turkey, which he founded during a successful first visit when the work of the Holy Spirit could be seen in a remarkable transformation of people's lives. Because the population was composed mainly of Celtic Gauls with relatively few Jews, Paul's missionary activity here is an example of his ability to communicate effectively and embrace ethnic, cultural, social and economic differences within a Christian community. No doubt his cosmopolitan background, education, experience, outlook, and fluency in Greek contributed to his success. Throughout his writing he shows affinity not only with Judaeic methods of interpreting Scripture, but also the Graeco-Roman rhetorical method of proposing a question which might be raised by objectors, and answering it in a presentation of argument characteristic of Hellenist culture. In Asia Minor, as well as in Galatia, he works in Ephesus, a major Aegean city dominated by Greek culture and the centre of the worship of Artemis, "the Diana of the Ephesians", where traders were annoyed that his influence threatened the profits they made from pagan shrines. In Mainland Greece he visits Philippi and Thessalonika in the northern district of

Macedonia, Athens, and Corinth in the southern district of Achaia. In his letter to the Romans he says that his mission has taken him as far west as Illyricum on the west coast of Croatia and announces his intention to complete the evangelisation of the northern Mediterranean world by going beyond Rome to Spain. (cf. *Ac* 19:24; *Rm* 15:24, 28.)

To the Galatians Paul recalls his vision of the glorified Christ on the road to Damascus. He had recognised the Son of God who became Man to redeem the world by his sacrificial death on the Cross, who atones for mankind's offence against God, and wins forgiveness with a restoration of sanctifying grace. All who believe in and obey Him are promised eternal life no matter what their race, class or sex. He is keenly aware of Isaiah's Suffering Servant, the Man of sorrows who carries our sufferings and is crushed for our sins in a punishment which brings us peace and heals our wounds. "The Lord burdened Him with the sins of all... He bore it humbly ...never opened His mouth like a Lamb that is led to the slaughter-house." (Cf. *Ga* 1:4, 16, 3:1-5, 20, 4:5; *Is* 53.)

Some Pharisaic Jewish Christians who had visited Galatia, told the Gentile converts that if they wanted to be justified by the redemption won by Christ on the Cross, they must first be converted to Judaeism before becoming Christians. Unless they were circumcised and were obedient to the Mosaic Law, faith in Christ would not be

enough to win them salvation and a share in the blessings
God promised to the descendants of Abraham. With
Apostolic authority Paul denounces these "false
brethren", because their teaching is contrary to the
universal nature of the Church founded by Christ, whose
own merits are without limit and whose own teaching is
continued by Peter and the Apostles

He puts the matter to the Galatians for their
consideration: "It is I Paul who tells you: if you allow
yourselves to be circumcised, Christ will be of no benefit
to you at all." Scripture reveals that faith in Christ
restores us to intimate and personal relationship with God
and membership of His people. From the time of
Abraham to that of Moses, justification was through faith
in the promises God made in the Covenant of which
circumcision was but a sign. From the time of Moses
until the arrival of Christ, justification was still through
faith in God's promises with the added obligation of the
Law He gave to Moses on Sinai. Of itself, this Law could
not redeem or justify, but now it is perfected by Christ so
that justification comes from faith in Him and observing
the Law of the Gospel.

Abraham himself gave the first evidence of
justification by the faith and trust in God which led to the
establishment of the Covenant. Because the Law did not
alter the Covenant, Jews and Gentiles alike experience
God's blessing and are all Abraham's descendants in

faith. The sign of circumcision does nothing to enhance the liberation from enslavement to sin which has been accomplished by Christ who is the consummation of the promises. After Paul made a return visit to the Galatians with the supportive judgement of the Council of Jerusalem, there were no further misunderstandings. The letter includes more information about his conversion and the start of his ministry, as well as the earliest statement about justification through faith in Christ. Directly and by allusion it teaches about the Blessed Trinity, union in Christ and with one another, the nature of the universal Church to which all become members through Baptism, the unity of doctrine, the pre-eminence of Peter, and Apostolic authority. (cf. *Gn* 17:3-9; *Mt* 5:17; *Ga* 1, 2, 2:15-20, 3:2-27, 4:6-19, 5:2, 6:15; *Ac* 10, 11, 16:4.)

Romans

By the middle of the first century AD, Rome had become home to many nationalities and creeds, and its million population included fifty thousand Jews with their synagogues and catacombs. Soon after Pentecost, the Jewish Christians began to preach the Good News in the synagogues, and Gentile believers established a number of house churches. There was a set-back in AD 49 when the emperor Claudius ordered all Jews to leave the city "because of disturbance at the instigation of Chrestus (sic)." (Suetonius, 'Claudius', 25:4.) This was less an

inaccurate reference to Our Lord than an indication of the
heated arguments about His Messianic credentials which
were disturbing the peace. Some Jews escaped expulsion
but the deportation of the majority significantly increased
the proportion of Gentiles in Roman Christian society.
Among those forced to leave were Aquila, a tent-maker
like Paul, and his wife Priscilla who joined his staff in
Corinth before moving to Ephesus and making their
home available as a church-meeting place. By the time he
wrote to the Romans they had returned to the capital after
Claudius' death in AD 54 when the edict was repealed,
and are admirable examples of the intrepid resilience and
mobility of the early Christians.

As the church in Rome flourished, it acquired a
prestige associated with the city's power and influence,
and because it was a special missionary field of Saint
Peter whose authority as Chief of the Twelve was
acknowledged by Jewish and Gentile Christians
throughout the empire. Paul had no wish to intrude upon
Peter's territory and, if the letter to the Hebrews which he
may not have written himself is excluded, this is the only
time he writes to a church not founded by himself.
Nevertheless, he has a responsibility as "Christ's minister
to the Gentiles", and it is understandable that a Roman
citizen should tell his old friends that he would like to
visit them before going to Spain. He apologises for his
presumption and, conscious of their reputation as a

"community of faith" and "the faithful flock" firm in its beliefs, his tone is respectful. Now that the Faith is reaching the ends of the earth, he can think of none better qualified to care for the propagation of true doctrine, now that he is going to new and unfamiliar territory. Paul does not mention Peter in Chapter 16, probably because he was temporarily absent from Rome, but this is no more unusual than Paul's own absences from the churches he himself founded.

His letter is addressed first and foremost to the Gentiles, and it must have been a relief to speak to an audience without opposition from zealous Judaeists. However, he takes the opportunity to repeat that God chooses to save all who have confidence in Him and makes no distinction between Jew and Gentile. "If your lips confess that Jesus is Lord and if you believe in your heart that God raised him from the dead, then you will be saved. By believing from the heart you are made righteous; by confessing with your lips you are saved." All have a share in God's own life, the sanctifying grace of salvation. This now flows to them again because Christ, by His Sacrifice, has once and for all reversed the sorry state of affairs which humanity, in the person of Adam, brought upon itself..

Whereas the letter to the Galatians was an immediate response to a particular pressing problem, this to the Romans is a presentation of his theological thinking and the tenets of the Faith after a three month period of careful reflection. The exposition is so comprehensive that it has been called his "Summa Theologica". St Augustine remarked that Paul "intended to teach the grace of the Gospel of Jesus Christ", and certainly the main theme of the letter is the sanctifying grace of salvation. He also summarises his teaching about the inability of fallen man to rise by his own efforts; God's will that we should be "justified", made holy and saved because His own righteousness seeks our return to original integrity; Redemption; salvation for all through faith in Christ in union with whom the soul is transformed to a holy and divine creation; the supernatural life and the all powerful efficacy of sanctifying grace which is the life of God Himself; the resolution of all problems by turning to Christ; the work of the Holy Spirit who makes good the frailty and deficiencies of human nature.

In the full statement of his vision of Christ and the community of faith, Paul gently corrects any misunderstandings which may have arisen from previous reactions to teaching. He is conscious of the supreme privilege enjoyed by the Jews in that God Himself took flesh as one of them. He has the highest expectations of their interests and theological knowledge as he considers the relationship between Judaeism and Christianity, and he balances the Hebrew interest in human reason with

Judaeic preference for the Law. Even though there may be occasional tension between Israelites and Gentiles, the Mosaic Law is the prefigurement of Christian Doctrine and is not in conflict with the new certainty that salvation is not just for a chosen race but for all.

Christ taught that it was right to pay tribute to Caesar because respect for the state as a feature of social life is in accord with God's plan. However, the early Christian proclamation that "Jesus is Lord" angered those who saw it as an assault on the assumed divinity of the emperor. Saint Peter drew attention to the persecution of Christians and found Rome's political, religious and economic climate so far from being a divine instrument of justice and peace that he called the place "Babylon", remembering Jerusalem's destruction at the hands of Romans and Babylonians. Paul offers the comfort that the community always functions as Christ's Mystical Body even when settling disputes or beset by a hostile society, and he gives practical advice about leading life according to the moral law in an indifferent, even threatening environment. (cf. *Ac* 18:1-4, 19:21; *1 Co* 16:19; *Rm* 1:10-3:24, 5, 6, 10:8-10, 11:13, 12:1-13, 14:1-15:33, 16:3; *Ph* 2:9-11; *1 P* 5:13; *Rv* 12-19; *Mk* 12:13-17.)

PHILIPPIANS C. AD 59

We remember how the conversions of Lydia, the slave-girl who was a fortune-teller, the gaoler and his family marked the beginning of the church in Philippi. The members supported Paul in his later travels, were sensitive to the rigours of his missionary activity, and always concerned for his well-being. The date of this letter to them is uncertain, but he says that he is "in chains for Christ", and his references to the soldiers who took turns to guard him in custody, and to the emperor's household, point to the first captivity in Rome when he was under house arrest. (cf. *Ph* 1:13, 4:22.) He is under no illusion about the opposition, danger, and likelihood of martyrdom, but remains certain of being with Christ after death. For the moment, however, he feels there is still work to be done for the churches who depend on him.

His tone is one of affectionate Christian friendship, with pastoral warmth and gratitude for all the help they have given him in bringing the Gospel to those who have not known Christ, and for their generous financial support. When Luke was writing the 'Acts of the Apostles', he stopped using "we" as soon as Paul and Silas left Philippi because he stayed on to "water" successfully what Paul had "planted". The "beloved Physician" has obviously transmitted to the faithful the care he had for his leader. (cf. *Ac* 16:40.)

Paul's love for this church in an empire colony leads him to think of it as an outpost of God's own heavenly Kingdom to which all Christians belong and owe allegiance. He develops the theme of justification, the righteousness which emanates from God and which is therefore in the nature of the soul as it responds to faith which is given freely because it cannot be merited. He warns against misguided teachers like those who had troubled the Galatians, and reflects on his own pilgrimage, his yearning to know Jesus above everything else, to share His sufferings, and emulate His death. It is in union with His Passion and being crucified with Him that humanity is created anew and shares in His glorious Risen Life. In the meantime, conscious of our need, we must work for our salvation in awe and with reverence, resolute in the face of conflict but always with confidence and joy in the Lord.

He asks them to be united in the work of evangelisation and exercise humility which fosters harmony. They must copy the behaviour of Our Lord which he describes in the "Christ Hymn", perhaps already familiar to the churches, and now quoted in profound faith and praise. In a beautifully eloquent veneration of His divinity, he draws from familiar doctrine the sublime lesson in humility. "In your own mind you must be the same as Christ Jesus. His state was divine, yet He did not cling to His equality with God but emptied Himself to assume the condition of a slave, and became as men are;

and being as men are, he was humbler yet, even to accepting death, death on a cross. But God raised Him high and gave Him the name which is above all other names, so that all beings in the heavens, on earth and in the underworld should bend the knee at the name of Jesus, and that every tongue should acclaim Jesus Christ as Lord, to the glory of God the Father." Paul gives us a glimpse of the mystery of Redemption and the completeness of the sacrifice of the human Christ who, in His desolation on the Cross, did not console Himself with the thought of Resurrection. His acceptance of the limitations and circumstances of human nature, and His obedience unto death contrast with the disobedience of Adam who thought he could have equality with God. (cf. *Ph* 1:23-29, 2:1-12, 3:1-21, 4:4ff; *Gn* 3:5.)

PHILEMON, COLOSSIANS, EPHESIANS C. AD 61-63

Paul wrote these three letters when he was under house arrest in Rome and there is a particular relationship between Colossians and Ephesians which are similar in circumstance to Galatians and Romans. He wrote to Colossae to warn the Christians there about a teaching which recommended a worship of celestial and cosmic "powers". He had to point out that even if these are the familiar angels of Judaeic tradition, they play only a preparatory and subordinate role in God's Plan of Salvation and His creation of a New Order in which Christ is all. The letter to the Ephesians is a more systematic consideration of Our Lord's supremacy.

Philemon

This is a brief, personal note to a valued friend and collaborator, written in circumstances similar to those affecting the Colossians and mentioning the same people. (cf. *Ph* 23, 24; *Col* 4:10.) A slave called Onesimus had absconded from his master Philemon and taken his grievance to Paul whom he hoped would mediate on his behalf. Paul was in a delicate situation because Philemon was a close friend, and Onesimus was the "child of captivity" whom he had converted while he was in prison, and was now therefore a "beloved brother". Moreover, a runaway slave was liable under the law to terrible punishment, even crucifixion. He sent him back with this letter in which, rather than exert his Apostolic authority, he opens with a graceful and diplomatic eulogy of Philemon's active faith and charity to which he appeals in asking mercy for Onesimus. He asks the master to welcome the slave as he would Paul himself and realise that, in the Divine Plan, the temporary loss of a slave brings the everlasting gain of a brother.

Paul hopes that Philemon will receive Onesimus as a brother in Christ and wonders if he might let him come back to help him while he is still "in the chains that the Good News has brought". In a pun on the Greek name "Onesimus" which means "useful, profitable", he quips, "He was of no use to you before, but he will be 'useful' to you now", perhaps hinting that a granting freedom to a slave would bring its own reward. He is obviously expecting his own early release at this stage because, before concluding with greetings from his colleagues who including Luke and Mark, he asks Philemon if he would arrange some lodgings for him. We do not know what happened, but the letter leaves no doubts about Paul's attitude to slavery, that "there is no distinction between slave and free man; there is only Christ." (*Col* 3:11.)

Colossians

The church at Colossae in Asia Minor, modern day Turkey, was founded by Epaphras, another of Paul's diligent assistants who in turn had been helped by Philemon who had provided accommodation for the church in his house. Most of the converts were Gentiles but there was a Judaeic element in the area which dated back to the Babylonian exile and dispersal of the Jews from their homeland. Paul was unfamiliar with this church and had not yet made a personal visit, so Epaphras visited him while he was in prison and reported the Colossians' wonderful progress in faith and charity, but it was not all good news. Certain teachers were purveying the philosophy that Christians should worship celestial beings and cosmic powers because they were intermediaries between God and the human race, crossing the divide between earth and heaven. It included a preoccupation with Judaeism, dietary detail, the ritual observance of holy days, and asceticism in search of visionary experiences, participation in the angels' worship of their Creator, and power over the invisible forces thought to control the world. The false teachers maintained that belief in Christ was only an introduction to the faith, the fulness of which was attained by the practices they advocated.

Paul condemns such teaching as more daemonic than divine, and foresees the dangers of an asceticism which enslaves rather than liberates, and an arrogant spirituality which is contemptuous of others. Accordingly, he wrote this letter to the Colossians which he asked Tychicus and Onesimus to deliver. He told them it should be read out first in the church which Epaphras had established in Laodicia which had a larger, more energetic population than Colossae. More forcefully than in any other letter he asserts the pre-eminent dignity of the Person of Jesus Christ who is "the first in every way" in time and in eternity, and in whom all perfection is found. He is the Divine Mediator who bridges the abyss between God and Man, between the finite and the infinite. He exists before Creation over which He has supreme spiritual and temporal authority. He is the Redeemer of the world and head of the Church which is His Mystical Body and, united to Him, man progresses to God and ultimate perfection. The prayer of the Church comes to mind: "Pour forth, we beseech You O Lord, Your grace into our hearts that we, to whom the Incarnation of Christ Your son was made known by the message of an angel may, by His Passion and Cross, be brought to the glory of His Resurrection."

Faith in Christ which is received in Baptism entitles a participation in His whole being and in everything that He accomplishes: the forgiveness of sin, reconciliation with the Father through the sacrificial death of the Son, escape from the tyranny of evil to the Kingdom of God, access to the treasury of wisdom and knowledge, hope for the world to come and the Beatific Vision, a share in the victory of the Resurrection and in the fulness of Christ the Son who is the perfect image of the Father. If we are clothed with Our Lord's "new nature", then forgiveness, love and peace come into their own and God is apparent in mutual respect, and in the service and justice which is exercised as if everything were done for the Lord. (cf. *Col* 3:10-4:1, also *Col* 1:7-27, 2:1-23.)

Ephesians

Our Lord's mission was first to the Jews because Israel's conversion was to be the pattern for all other nations. That the Gentiles were not prepared to wait, however, is manifest in the absolute confidence of the Roman centurion who asked Jesus to heal his son, and in the persistence of the Syrophoenician mother who sought help for her daughter who was plagued by an unclean spirit. These were signs of the Kingdom of God's arrival, and Jesus said he had not encountered such faith in Israel. As the number of Gentile followers grew, He ministered to them and demolished barriers by sharing the lives of the tax-collectors and other "sinners" who were ostracised by Judaeic society. (cf. *Mk* 5, 7:24-30; *Lk* 7:1-10.)

This letter reads more like an encyclical intended for a group of churches than a response to a specific local issue. Paul is still a prisoner in Rome as he expands on a subject already mentioned in Colossians. He gives thanks for the love which God has for all His people and contemplates the empire founded by Christ, the divine Redeemer of Jew and Gentile. He recalls the former hostile blockades like the wall in the Temple which separated the Court of the Gentiles from the inner sanctum, an architectural misinterpretation of holiness which was thought to protect God's elect from those who were considered to be excluded from the Covenant. Then there was the fence which the Mosaic Law had erected around Israel, forbidding intermarriage and the breaking of bread with Gentiles. We have seen that the Council of Jerusalem had to resolve the differences between Jewish Christians who were circumcised and observed the Mosaic law, and the uncircumcised Gentile converts who were not so obliged. Following Our Lord's example, Paul maintained that Gentile observance of the Mosaic Law would be tantamount to denying what God has accomplished in Christ.

Redeemed mankind, united as members of His Body, progresses from earth to heaven as He, the Head, distributes the vital force of sanctifying grace. He nourishes the Body's growth and perfects its development as He brings God's eternal plan for the world's salvation to its fruitful consummation. He is the bearer of Good News who brings peace to far and near and, by His death on the Cross, effects reconciliation with God, and with those previously divided by the rules and decrees of the Law. All are now united in His one Body, the Church which He loves as a husband loves his bride, with unique intimacy and without condition. He has surrendered Himself to save her and washes away all sin in the waters of Baptism. No one is a foreign visitor and "all are part of a building that has the Apostles and the prophets for its foundation with Christ Jesus Himself for its main cornerstone... All grow into one, holy temple in the Lord... built into a house where God lives in the Spirit."

Paul again sees the Church won by Christ through His atoning sacrifice as a Mystical Body subject to the Head who nourishes her. She is ONE body with one Head, and is one in faith, doctrine, government and worship. She is HOLY because her members are sanctified and saved by her Founder, the all holy God who commissions her to teach a holy doctrine and provide all the means to holiness. She is CATHOLIC because all human beings who inhabit the universe "are citizens like all the saints and part of God's household" (2:19), and her incomparable teaching mission is to them for whose benefit she is entrusted with the way of salvation. She is APOSTOLIC, for she is the temple founded on the Apostles through whose unbroken pastoral succession she preserves their traditions and the doctrines they learned directly from Jesus Christ. She is the VISIBLE society which Christ wishes to be taught by the Apostles, Evangelists and Shepherds He appoints.

When Adam sinned all were lost, but through Christ's merits members of His Body are saved. Those who believe and seek to believe in Him share His victory over sin and the powers of darkness, and the Holy Spirit who dwells in them guarantees their inheritance. Paul's concentration on Our Lord's continuing activity as Head of the Mystical Body has found recent expression in the papal encyclical 'Mystici Corporis Christi', 'The Mystical Body of Christ'(Pope Pius XII, 1943). "Christ is in us and we are in Christ through His Spirit whom He imparts to us and through whom He so acts within us that any divine effect operated in our souls by the Holy Spirit must be said to be operated in us also by Christ... It is also due to the communication of the Spirit of Christ that all the gifts, virtues, and miraculous powers found so eminently and abundantly in the Head which is their source, stream into all the members of the Church and in them are perfected daily... Consequently the Church becomes, as it were, the fulness and completion of the Redeemer, Christ in the Church being in some sense brought to complete achievement... Christ, the Mystical Head and the Church which, like another Christ represents His person on earth, together contribute one "new man, joining Heaven and earth in the continuation of the saving work of the Cross." (78)

Paul uses physiology, perhaps learned from Luke, his "beloved Physician", to teach that Christ is supreme in every respect, present everywhere in the Church which grows and develops in charity. The life, energy, merit and perfection of the members comes from the grace which flows from the Head and Saviour of the Body, and he advises them how members of the Mystical Body best serve and strengthen one another. "Even if you are angry, you must not sin. Never let the sun set on your anger... Guard against foul talk; let your words be for the improvement of others, as occasion offers, and do good to your listeners, otherwise you will only be grieving the Holy Spirit of God who has marked you with His seal for you to be set free when the day comes. Never have grudges against others, or lose your temper, or raise your voice to anybody, or call each other names, or allow any part of spitefulness. Be friends with one another, and kind, forgiving each other as readily as God forgave you in Christ. Try then to imitate God, as children of His that He loves, and follow Christ by loving as He loved you, giving Himself up in our place as a fragrant offering and a sacrifice to God." (*Eph* 4:26-5:2 and cf. 1:3-2:22, 3:1-21, 4:7-5:21, 6:9-11; *Is* 52:7-19; *Ga* 3:7-14.)

1 TIMOTHY, TITUS, 2 TIMOTHY C. AD 64-5

Paul is in prison for the second time and, knowing that execution is inevitable, wants to offer his final words of advice. He writes to two of his most loyal collaborators on the subject of church leadership and its details like the appointment, remuneration and discipline of elders and ministers, the transmission of sound doctrine to support Faith, liturgical worship, the role of women, and the care of widows which was so important in an age when the death of a husband generally left a wife destitute. The letters have become known as the "Pastoral Letters" and, although sent to individuals, can be received by Christian communities in every era, as the writer gives examples of leadership performance and structure which remain applicable to progress, institutional health, unity and ecumenical discussion.

Under the leadership of Timothy and Titus, their respective churches at Ephesus and Crete had so prospered that they had become an integral part of society. Unfortunately, some Jewish teachers anxious to make money by attracting a discipleship, were going round forbidding marriage, condemning certain food, and eroding the faith of some of the church members. The disharmony they created in the church community affected its ability to cohere with and influence society, especially since the troublemakers were trying to disseminate a philosophy which was alien to the traditions of the empire. Paul dismisses the prohibitions because they arise from the invalid assumptions that marriage and certain foods are somehow impure. He has no objection to abstaining from marriage and commends the celibate life of those whom God calls to serve Him in this way. Fasting, too, is admirable when used to control appetites and the senses. "Everything God has created is good and no food is to be rejected, provided grace is said. Have nothing to do with godless myths and old wives' tales." He wants people "to behave in God's family, that is in the Church of the living God which upholds the truth and keeps it safe," and "to lift their hands reverently in prayer without anger or argument."

To ward off the dangers which he anticipates, Paul says that the truth must be preserved and cherished by the Church who explains its hidden mysteries and nourishes the moral life which is of its essence. She is the fortress against error and, guided by the Holy Spirit, she continues and guarantees the teaching of Christ. To do this she needs carefully selected ministers of holy life and high ideals to guard the deposit of faith and hand on to the community the sound doctrine she has received through the Apostles. He urges the leaders to hold fast to this teaching and choose fellow-workers who will transmit it faithfully. He asks Timothy and Titus to have the greatest care for everything that has been entrusted to them and to have nothing to do with "pointless philosophical discussion and a divisive presumption of knowledge which is no knowledge at all." In their dealings with false teachers he tells them to "remember the good news that I carry, Jesus Christ risen from the dead; if we hold firm we shall reign with Him" and, in proposing a worthy manner of life, he offers as a model the record of his own teachings and suffering.

Paul's intention has been to foil attempts to undermine the Christian apostolate, but there are reminders of other matters of faith about which he has written in previous letters. "God wants everyone to be saved and reach full knowledge of the truth. For there is only one God, and there is only one Mediator between God and mankind, Himself a man, Christ Jesus who has offered Himself as a ransom for all. The theme of the loving obedience of Our Lord who gave His life to redeem us is developed. "He sacrificed Himself... to set us free from all wickedness and to purify a people so that they should be His very own and would have no ambition but to do good." He adds how appropriate it is that we should pray for all the living and the dead, make no distinction between the circumstances of one's state of life and the advancement of salvation and perfection, appreciate how effective is the apostolate of good example, and understand the qualities required in candidates for the ministry.

As Paul awaits his martyrdom, he looks back on the trials and sufferings of his mission, and forward to the "crown of righteousness", the vision of God which his Lord, the just Judge will give him. Eternal life is the reward of merit but it is God's gift freely given, for without His grace there can be no merit. He shivers in his prison and asks Timothy to bring him a winter cloak when he next comes to visit. During the preliminaries of his trial no one came forward to say a good word for him but, in the course of conducting his own defence, he still took the opportunity to preach the Gospel. The passing of sentence has been postponed for the time being, he has "been rescued from the lion's mouth", but he has little hope of a final acquittal. In his fond and final farewells, he mentions Linus who, according to Eusebius and tradition, succeeded Peter as Bishop of Rome. Characteristically and appropriately, he signs off with a doxology to the Christ whom he has served so selflessly and valiantly, from whom comes the grace of delivery and salvation. "To Him be glory for ever and ever. Amen." (cf. *1 Tm* 1:6-15, 2:5, 3:10-16, 4:8-16, 5:22, 6:3-21; *Tt* 1:5, 2:1-14; *2 Tm* 1:8-18, 2:2-23, 3:1f, 4:1-22.)

HEBREWS C. AD 65

Paul writes to the Jewish community in Jerusalem which included some converts from the Levitical priesthood. They had been facing persecution and he was concerned that if their confidence wavered they might return to Judaeism. He urges them to hold fast to the faith so that they will not share the fate of those who failed to reach the Promised Land. He wants them to rekindle their first fervour and imitate the perseverance of the Apostles. He does not mention his own name, doubtless out of reverence for Christ, the Apostle of the Hebrews upon whose supreme authority he would not encroach, but he has been commissioned by Him to speak to the Hebrews and asks that his words be received in the spirit of kindness with which they are sent. He offers the Roman world a summary of Christian belief in what reads like a formal dissertation to which personal touches have been added. Paul's assumption that his audience is familiar with Temple rites and terminology indicates that its destruction in AD 70 by the emperor Titus after the Jewish rebellion was still to come, and the mention of Timothy's release after his imprisonment following the fire of Rome in AD 64, help a rough calculation of the letter's date. His own final captivity had evidently not begun because he hopes to see them soon and sends greetings from "all the saints" in Italy where he seems to have stopped on his return from Spain before turning his attention once more to Jerusalem and the East.

The Jewish philosopher, Philo of Alexandria (BC 30-AD 40), used allegory to interpret the first five books of the Old Testament, also known as the 'Torah', which embody the Law given to Moses, and the body of Jewish religious literature. He proposed the compatibility of Greek philosophy and Scripture by, for example, comparing Abraham's journey from Ur to the Promised Land to the Platonic vision of the soul's progress from the dark shadows of the physical world to the radiant light of the Creator. So too, the experiences of the Patriarchs and Israel's privileged status are aligned with the Platonic opinion that God is encountered not only through His words in the sacred Scriptures, but also in the achievements of human beings who manifest the glory of Him who made them.

Paul understands Philo's influence on Alexandrian and other Jews who appreciated their heritage as a blending of biblical tradition and Hellenist philosophy. He makes the Platonic distinction between the ideal and limited worlds when he presents Our Lord as perfection compared to the former religious dispensation. This familiarity with Greek philosophy and uncertainty about the date, led some to attribute authorship to Apollos, but this underestimates Paul's background, education, and intellect. Certainly, over the next thirty years Pope St Clement, St Polycarp, and St Justin never doubted that the letter was from Paul, and it was considered of such theological importance that the earliest canons placed it immediately after Romans.

Paul remembers how Noah, Jacob, Joseph and the Israelites never lost confidence in God and His promises despite the most dreadful setbacks, and were faithful unto death even though they were not to see the ultimate promise fulfilled in Christ. The God of the Hebrew religion graciously calls Himself the God of Abraham, Isaac and Jacob, and reveals His plan of salvation first through His Prophets and then most gloriously through His Son whose teaching He affirms, while the Holy Spirit bestows His gifts and graces. Paul then reviews the great themes of Christian faith and hope described by St Thomas Aquinas as "the excellence of Christ". He uses the biblical tradition to show how God's preparatory revelation in the Old Covenant becomes a New and everlasting Covenant which perfects the relationship between God and His people. All is accomplished in His anointed Son, Jesus Christ, the agent and Redeemer of creation whom the angels adore. For a while He made Himself inferior to them so that He could be identified with His human brothers and sisters who, through His obedience, passion and death, He now leads to holiness.

Paul points out that the sacrifices offered by the Levitical priesthood were limited in that they did not

sanctify the people, but Jesus offers the perfect sacrifice
of Himself, once and for all, and He purifies the inner
conscience. The primary agent, guarantor of faith, and
model of humanity now sits vindicated at God's right
hand as supreme High Priest, Revealer and Ruler whose
obedience is now exalted to divine dignity. The Jewish
high priest went into what was only an earthly tabernacle
to offer sacrifice on the atonement day, but Jesus enters
Heaven to return the people to His Father. The Good
Shepherd and gate of the Sheepfold seals the New
Covenant with His Blood, takes us into the Holy of
Holies and opens the way to the Throne of Grace. The
eternal royal Priest who has no need of sacrifices, rules
the House which Moses foresaw that God would build of
the New Covenant people.

Paul readily admits that the People of God who
compose His Church will face suffering and trials similar
to those experienced by the Israelites, and they will be
challenged when they proclaim the truth about the nature
of God and His intentions for His people. However, faith
in the eternal realities of Our Lord's sacrifice, and as the
foundation of daily life, gives them entry to God's House
where they are sustained in their endeavours to win new
life in His Kingdom. Though sinless He faced
temptations, and He understands the frailty of His
brothers and sisters. "The limits of their faults and
weaknesses do not obscure the vision of His glory or the

peace He has promised." (Prayer of the Church.) They
have only to turn to Him and He helps them with His
mercy and grace, for in Him there is salvation. Paul
leaves us with his continuing prayer "that the God of
Peace who brought Our Lord Jesus back from the dead...
may make you ready to do His will in any kind of good
action, and turn us all into whatever is acceptable to
Himself through Christ Jesus, to whom be glory for ever
and ever. Amen"

ACKNOWLEDGEMENTS

CTS kindly acknowledges quotations from:

The Jerusalem Bible, Darton, Longman & Todd, London, 1974.
The Divine Office, Collins, London, 1974.
Westminster Hymnal, Burns, Oates & Washbourne, London, 1948.

Bibliography

Catholic Commentary on the Holy Scripture, Thomas Nelson & Sons, London, 1951.

Cambridge Companion to the Bible, Cambridge University Press, 1997.

A History of Christianity, Owen Chadwick, Weidenfeld & Nicholson, London, 1995.

The Story of Christianity, M. Collins & M. Price, Dorling Kindersley, London, 1999.

Commentary on the Whole Bible, M. Henry, Harper Collins, London, 1960.

The Complete Bible Handbook, John Bowker, Dorling Kindersley, London, 1998.

Catechism of the Catholic Church, Geoffrey Chapman, London, 1994.

What Saint Paul Really Said, Tom Wright, Lion Books, 1997.

Informative Catholic Reading

We hope that you have enjoyed reading this booklet.

If you would like to find out more about CTS booklets - we'll send you our free information pack and catalogue.

Please send us your details:

Name ....

Address ....

....

....

Postcode ....

Telephone..

Email ....

Send to: CTS, 40-46 Harleyford Road,
            Vauxhall, London
            SE11 5AY

Tel: 020 7640 0042
Fax: 020 7640 0046
Email: info@cts-online.org.uk

 **CTS**